Relationships 101

By
Drs. Les and Leslie Parrott

Honor Books
Tulsa, Oklahoma

Unless otherwise indicated, all Scripture quotations are taken from *The Living Bible*, copyright © 1971. Used by permission of Tyndale House Publishers, Inc., Wheaton, Illinois 60189. All rights reserved.

Relationships 101
ISBN 1-56292-450-8
Copyright © 1998 by Les and Leslie Parrott
Center for Relationship Development
Seattle Pacific University
Seattle, Washington 98119

Published by Honor Books
P.O. Box 55388
Tulsa, Oklahoma 74155

Introduction

No matter how some people may blanch at the idea, sooner or later everyone realizes that human beings aren't designed to "go it alone." If that were not the case, "solitary confinement" might be considered some great resort activity, rather than punishment for our planet's most dastardly criminals.

Indeed, life demands that all human beings, great and small, must find their way through the maze of human relationships. Our words, attitudes, and behaviors, like ripples on a pond, affect the lives of every person with whom we come in contact.

Leslie and I have made the study of relationships our life work. In so doing, we hope to gain insights for ourselves and offer help to others who are plodding along in the midst of the maze. Relationships 101 contains the best fruit of our endeavors, as well as words of wisdom from other sources that we have gathered along the way. We hope you will find yourself strengthened as you continue your journey.

Family

Celebrating the Ties that Bind

_____

*I*n truth, most of what we
think, feel, say, and do
is in response to the home
where we grew up.

_____

7he family is a classroom
where we learn the skills
that will one day enable us
to live on the outside.

Sometimes you get so far away
from your family, you think you're
outside its influence forever.
Then before you figure out
what's happening, it's right there
beside you, pulling the strings.

Peter Collier

———

*W*hen I was a boy of fourteen,
my father was so ignorant I could
hardly stand to have the old man around. But
when I got to be twenty one, I was astounded
at how much he had learned in seven years.

Mark Twain

———

The family you come from
isn't as important as the family
you're going to have.

Ring Lardner

To bring up a child in the way he should go,
travel that way yourself
once in a while.

Josh Billings

(Henry Wheeler Shaw)

---

*T*he greatest thing in family life is to take a hint when a hint is intended –and not to take a hint when a hint isn't intended.

Robert Frost

Family

———

*A*ll happy families are like one another;
each unhappy family is unhappy
in its own way.

Leo Tolstoy

———

13

---

*F*amily is a link to our past
and a bridge to our future.

Alex Haley

Relationship Booster!

*A*t your next family gathering, make an effort to compliment each family member for at least one thing during the course of the day. Some compliments may be more challenging than others and the particularly difficult ones may require advanced planning. No matter how great the effort, the results of this exercise always exceed expectations. You will be amazed by the immediate improvement in family relations when you begin to accentuate the positive and let others know they are valued.

Questions to Ponder

- How was love expressed in your family while you were growing up?

- How often were the words "I love you" spoken?

- How often do you express your love for the significant people in your life?

Questions to Ponder

- In what specific ways has your family of origin shaped your personality, your career choices, your relationships, and your values?

- Do you find it difficult to acknowledge the influence your family has had on your life and choices?

Questions to Ponder

James 1:19 says, "Be quick to listen and slow to speak." That can be a tough assignment, especially with family members.

- Do you believe it is necessary to set aside time to listen to each member of your family?

- Do you often find yourself giving unsolicited advice to family members?

Relationship Booster!

*O*ne of the great illusions of our age is that love is
self-sustaining. It is not. Love takes time.
List the names of your immediate family members.
For one month, keep track of how much time
you spend with each person on the list.
You may be surprised by the results.

Relationship Buster!

*F*amilies are often better at *forgiving* than *forgetting!*

Relating to family members on the basis of
who they were rather than *who they are*
will always result in disharmony.

Friends

✍

Prospering in Fair Weather and Foul

---

*T*his communicating of a man's self to his
friend works two contrary effects,
for it redoubleth joys, and
cutteth griefs in half.

Francis Bacon

———

*I*n prosperity our friends know us,
in adversity we know our friends.

Churton Collins

———

———

The only reward of virtue is virtue;
the only way to have a friend is to be one.

Ralph Waldo Emerson

———

The holy passion of friendship is of so sweet
and steady and loyal and enduring a nature
that it will last through a whole lifetime,
if not asked to lend money.

Mark Twain

———

*E*ven strong friendships require
watering, or they are sure to
shrivel up and blow away.

———

Did You Know?

Friendship can help us ward off depression,
boost our immune systems, lower our
cholesterol levels, increase our odds of
surviving coronary disease,
and keep stress hormones in check.

I do not believe that friends are
necessarily the people you like best,
they are merely the people
who got there first.

Peter Ustinov

$\mathcal{D}$o not use a hatchet
to remove a fly from your friend's forehead.

Chinese Proverb

---

*I*t takes a lot more grace to enjoy
the successes of our friends than it does
to comfort them when disaster strikes.

———

You can always tell a real friend;
when you've made a fool of yourself,
he doesn't feel you've done a permanent job.

Laurence J. Peter

———

_____

Love thy neighbor as thyself,
but choose your neighborhood.

Louise Beal

_____

―――――

*G*enuine friendship cannot exist where one of the parties is unwilling to hear the truth and the other is equally indisposed to speak it.

Cicero

―――――

---

*N*othing but nothing matters more in friendship than being true!

———

*W*oe to him who is alone when he falls
and has not another to lift him up.

Ecclesiastes 4:10

———

---

*F*riendship is like money,
easier made than kept.

Samuel Butler

_____

Often we have no time for our friends but all the time in the world for our enemies.

Leon Uris

_____

———

*W*hen you prosper, loyal friends
applaud your successes
and cheer you on without envy.

———

Friends

―――

Comfortable friends often suffer the most
from busyness and neglect.

―――

---

*P*eople with deep and lasting friendships
may be introverts, extroverts, young, old,
dull, intelligent, homely, good looking;
but the one characteristic they always
have in common is openness.

Alan Loy McGinnie

Friends

The friends we keep the longest are often the
friends who forgave us the most.

The solid commitment between faithful friends is established by thousands of seemingly insignificant commitments over the long haul.

Did You Know?

Having a good laugh with friends
stimulates endorphins,
the brain's natural painkillers.

---

*L*aughter is not at all a bad beginning
for a friendship, and it is far
the best ending for one.

Oscar Wilde

Friends

Relationship Booster!

Alexander Graham Bell patented the telephone in 1876. Use it!
Make of list of five friends you have not spoken with in at least a year
and call one, just to talk, each month for the next five months.

During the sixth month, create a second list.

Don't be concerned if your second list looks a lot like your first.

Word to the Wise: Don't let a misplaced telephone number
stand in your way. Most people aren't in hiding and can be
found easily if you are willing to make the effort .

---

*O*n the road between the homes of friends, grass does not grow.

Norwegian Proverb

————

Faithful are the wounds of a friend.

Proverbs 27:6

————

Questions to Ponder

- What characteristics do you look for in a friend?

- Do you consider yourself a true friend?

Relationship Booster!

*H*ow long has it been since you spoke with
the people who live right next door?

It's often best to prime the pump by showing some simple gesture
of kindness: shoveling the snow from your neighbor's driveway,
mowing all or part of your neighbor's lawn, sharing home-baked
goods, passing along fresh produce from the garden.

Use these opportunities to engage your neighbors in conversation,
and watch as friendship is born.

Remember: Do more *listening* than *talking!*

Relationship Buster!

*B*reaking a confidence is one of the easiest ways
to lose a good friend.

Cover your friendships with *implied* confidentiality.
That means unless you are told otherwise, conversations
with good friends are "for your ears only."

Romance

Discovering the Promise of Love

———

*E*very romance runs the risk of fading.
Let me rephrase that:
Romance always fades!

——— No it doesn't!

*H*ealthy, rewarding relationships
are built on the following:
a strong sense of personal identity,
a thriving self-esteem,
a personal sense of purpose,
the ability to commit to things outside oneself,
mutual respect,
good, old-fashioned courage.

---

*I*f you fail to address your hurts from
previous relationships
and seek healing, you are destined to replay
the pain again and again
in future relationships.

———————

*I*mmature love says,
"I love you because I need you."
Mature love says,
"I need you because I love you."

Erich Fromm

———————

———

Love gives itself; it is not bought.

Henry Wadsworth Longfellow

———

---

*T*he right person can not and
will not make your life complete.
Once you have accepted that fact,
you will be eligible for a happy,
fulfilling relationship.

———

*O*nce a spark of attraction catches flame,
it can quickly become a raging fire
of unreasonable passion.
It's best not to make decisions
while engulfed in its heat!

———

———

$\mathcal{P}$assion, though a bad regulator,
is a powerful spring.

Ralph Waldo Emerson

———

———

*W*hen you say, "If this person needs me,
I'll be complete,"
you are reducing others to projects
on your relationship resume.

———

———————

*L*ove built on beauty,
soon as beauty,
dies.

John Donne

———————

———

*P*assion, intimacy, and commitment are the
hot, warm, and cold ingredients
in love's recipe.

———

———

*G*ratitude is one of the best-kept secrets
of happy dating relationships.

———

———

Dating has its own spin cycle.
The excitement, anticipation, expectations,
dashed hopes, demands, and pressure
can leave you spinning at dizzying speeds.

———

*C*ommitment looks toward a future
that cannot be seen,
and promises to be there.

———

*C*ommitment is not as difficult as it seems,
but it does require a cool head
and a steadfast heart.

———

Did You Know?

Men focus primarily on achievement
and women focus primarily
on relationships.

———

*T*he affections are like lightening:
You cannot tell where they will
strike till they have fallen.

Jean Baptiste Lacordaire

———

———

*I*nfatuation has its place:
But as anyone who has been in love
can tell you, it's difficult to live on top
of the mountain day after day.

———

Young love is a flame; very pretty, very hot and fierce but still only light and flickering. The love of the older and disciplined heart is as coals, deep burning, unquenchable.

Henry Ward Beecher

A man falls in love through his eyes,
a woman through her ears.

Woodrow Wyatt

———

*L*ove is an act of
endless forgiveness,
a tender look which becomes a habit.

Peter Ustinov

———

———

*T*oo many unsteady couples
wobble to the alter–
as if getting there is the point.

———

_____

*W*hat are the four most intimidating words
in a couple's vocabulary?
"We need to talk."

_____

---

*B*e forewarned:
A date is often a show case,
designed to show only the best side
and conceal the shortcomings.

———

Some people stay in an
unhappy dating relationship because
even a bad relationship can
provide a sense of security.

———

———

*L*ove must be learned, and learned
again and again;
there is no end to it.

Katherine Anne Porter

———

———

Love is a strange mixture of opposites:
Affection and anger,
excitement and boredom,
stability and change,
restriction and freedom.

———

———

*C*ommitment creates a
small island of certainty
in the swirling waters of uncertainty.

———

----

*C*ommitment serves as a mooring
when passion burns low
and turbulent times and fierce
impulses overtake us.

---

*B*ecome the kind of person
you are looking for.

People who throw kisses
are hopelessly lazy.

Bob Hope

---

*T*is better to have loved and lost than
to be stuck with a real loser for the rest
of your entire, miserable existence!

Hallmark coffee mug slogan

The best divorce is the one you get *before* you get married.

Folk saying

———

Nothing takes the taste out of peanut butter
quite like unrequited love.

Charlie Brown

———

———————

*H*eaven has no rage like
love to hatred turned.

William Congreve

———————

Every dating relationship will include
terrible, rotten, no-good days.
During these bad times, you will learn what
your prospective mate is made of.

―――――

*I*nstead of trying to make
someone into the ideal partner,
pour your energies into making yourself
a better person.

―――――

Some couples go into marriage
thinking they will agree
on everything simply because
while they were dating,
they *seemed* to agree on everything.

———

$\mathcal{D}$ating is tough!
Trying to forge an authentic relationship
amidst all the romantic hype is
a daunting proposition.

———

––––––

*W*e say "opposites attract"
because many people are drawn to
partners who complement them–those
who complete them in some way.

––––––

———

For women only:
You can talk to the man in your life about
your feelings, fears, and experiences,
but don't expect him to listen with
the same vigilance you would expect
from your girlfriends.

———

———

*F*or men only:
It isn't likely that the woman in your life
will fully understand your "need for space"
or be willing to romanticize
your independence.

———

_____

*J*f I am attached to another person because
I cannot stand on my own two feet,
he or she may be a life saver, but the
relationship is not one of love.

Erica Fromm

_____

$\mathcal{B}$eing a woman is a terribly difficult task
since it consists principally in
dealing with men.

Joseph Conrad

————

*R*elationships are exhausting until we figure out how to direct our energies in ways that [the opposite gender] can truly appreciate. Then we all win.

John Gray

————

———

*T*he half life of romantic love is
about three months,
after which you have only half
the amount of romantic feelings
you started out with.

———

———

Some Cinderellas are longing
for a Prince Charming to come along,
turn their world inside out,
and make everything bad go away.

That's the trouble with fiction!

———

———

$\mathcal{M}$en and women, women and men,
it will never work.

Erica Jong

———

Did You Know?

The number one trait that Americans, both men and women, claim they look for first in a prospective mate is: *A sense of humor!*

Did You Know?

The number two trait that Americans, both men and women, claim to be the second thing they look for in a prospective mate is: *Intelligence*.

It's wise to pay less attention to
your date's physical characteristics
and more attention to how he or she
responds when things go wrong.

———

*W*hen men and women agree,
it is only in their conclusions;
their reasons are always different.

George Santayana

———

*T*he problem women run into when they try to explore men's emotional needs is that men don't want women to explore their emotional needs!

———

*W*hat women want:
To be loved, to be listened to, to be desired,
to be trusted, and sometimes, just to be held.

*W*hat men want:
Tickets for the world series.

Dave Barry

———

Relationship Booster!

*D*o you know who you are in love with?
You may think you know. But do you really?

Many people base the quality of their romantic relationships on those things that one day will matter least. Lasting love is based on connections made deep in the heart—primarily shared values and beliefs.

When you feel yourself falling for someone, take the time to ask important questions and listen with your heart.

It isn't necessary to become uncomfortably deep.
Try the following:

• What is your greatest goal in life?

• If you could change the world, where would you begin?

• What is your image of the ideal family?

• What characteristic do you dislike most in a person?

Did You Know?

Roughly half the women polled in a recent survey said they would be willing to cry to get their way.

Only 20 percent of the men said they would do so.

Did You Know?

The number one reason college students seek counseling is for problems in their relationships.

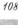

Did You Know?

*W*hen asked to choose between wealth, attractiveness, or a good personality in a relationship, the vast majority of men and women said they would choose a good personality.

Questions to Ponder

*A*n ancient Chinese proverb says,
"Patience is power.
With time and patience,
the mulberry leaf becomes silk."

- How can patience increase the beauty
and value of a dating relationship?
- How much time do you spend
listening on a date?

Questions to Ponder

In life, we often get what we want most!
For example, deeper and more meaningful
relationships can be achieved by setting aside
the fulfillment of self-centered desires.

• What do you want most?
• Are you willing to put the goals and desires
of another person before your own?

Questions to Ponder

- Why is truth so fundamental to love?
  - Can love survive without truth?

Relationship Booster!

*M*ake a list of the characteristics you like most
in the person you are dating.
You can present the list on a special occasion or simply
drop them one at a time along the road to romance.

You might want to consider doing both!

When you make a habit of accentuating the positive,
love almost always grows faster and stronger
for both the presenter and the receiver.

Relationship Buster!

*C*omparisons are deadly!

When you fail to appreciate the uniqueness
of each person you date,
you build unrealistic expectations in your own mind and
insurmountable obstacles in the mind of the other person.
The past relationship whether good or bad
will quickly encroach on the present.

Marriage

Walking in Love for a Lifetime

―――――

*W*hen the scales of a relationship are unbalanced—one person is always giving and one is always receiving— both will eventually feel cheated.

―――――

———

Spirituality is to marriage
what yeast is to bread.
Ultimately, your spiritual commitment
will determine whether your
marriage rises successfully
or falls disappointingly flat.

———

*I*t's no mistake that
maturity and *matrimony*
come from the same Latin word.

*R*elationships are ultimately
a deep, mysterious, and
unfathomable spiritual endeavor.

---

*L*ove does not consist in
gazing at each other but in looking
together in the same direction.

Antoine DeSaint-Exupery

$\mathcal{D}$o not let the sun go down
while you are still angry.

Ephesians 4:26

———

$\mathcal{M}$arriage means giving up a
carefree lifestyle and coming
to terms with new limits.
It means unexpected inconveniences!

———

————

*F*orgiveness in marriage can only heal when
the focus is on what our spouses *do*,
rather than who they *are*.

————

———

*W*ise up!
The little things you do now–
without thinking–will cut
a life-long groove in your relationship.

———

———

*L*ove is like a tennis match;
you'll never win consistently until
you learn to serve well.

Dan P. Herod

———

———

*C*ompliments feel good–
both to give and to receive.

———

———

A happy marriage cannot survive
the cancer of resentment.
Like self pity and blame,
it eats at the human spirit
and kills the capacity for joy.

———

————

*H*appy couples *decide* to be happy.
In spite of the troubles life deals them,
they make happiness a habit.

————

$\mathcal{T}$he habit of happiness is an inside job.

———

No one can make another person unhappy.
You can't often control your circumstances,
but you can control your attitude
toward those circumstances.

———

———

*M*arital unhappiness is never
caused by only one person.
That's why therapists
focus not on *who* is wrong,
but *what* is wrong.

———

*L*iving happily ever after only works if
you *make* it work.

Marriage

---

*S*uccessful couples take the raw materials of marriage–the good and bad they bring together as persons–and create their own unique and lasting bond.

———

The deepest kind of sharing can take place
only when there is no fear of rejection.

———

———

The more couples focus on
what they have in common,
the deeper intimacy grows.

———

———

*R*esentment is to relationships
as cancer is to the body.
At first it is small and imperceptible,
but over time it grows larger and
spreads its poison throughout.

———

———

*F*aithfulness is like a multifaceted jewel,
exhibiting a complex combination
of interrelated dimensions
such as trust, commitment, truth, loyalty,
valuing, and care.

———

*M*arriages can never be perfect
because people are never perfect!

*W*hat we anticipate seldom occurs;
what we least expect generally happens–
especially in marriage!

Relationship Booster!

*P*raying together is a powerful
and positive element in any relationship.

In marriage, it can truly result in increased understanding
and a deeper sense of oneness.

Agree on a time to pray together for just five minutes each day.
Lay aside personal business for mutual concerns,
and each should encourage the other to pray aloud.

———

Love grows less exciting
with time for the same reason
the second run on a fast toboggan
is less exciting than the first.

———

———

$\mathcal{I}$n the measure that young passion recedes,
the vacancy is replaced with a deeper,
more abiding sense of
intimacy, care, and co-creativity.
As the flame fades,
deep-burning coals emerge.

———

---

*W*hat is the most dramatic loss
experienced in a new marriage?
The idealized image you have of your partner.

Did You Know?

*E*very day 8 Americans over the age of 65
marry for the *first* time.

Did You Know?

A major predictor of marital satisfaction is the husband's independence from his parents.

Did You Know?

A survey found that 75 percent of those polled were more tolerant of their pets' misdeeds than those of their spouses or children.

Did You Know?

Women tend to be more distressed when their spouses are involved with emotional infidelity.

Men are more distressed when their spouses are involved with physical infidelity.

Did You Know?

Relationships that lead to marriage usually begin with the help of a third party, such as a family member or mutual friend.

Questions to Ponder

It is said that men "report talk"
and women "rapport talk."
Do you find this to be true?

Questions to Ponder

When was the last time your spouse took
priority over a project at work
or an "important" deadline?

Relationship Booster!

$\mathcal{M}$any people fail to express their love to the very person they love the most.

Test yourself.

Do you express your love and appreciation for your spouse:

- More than once a day?
- More than once a week?
- More than once a month?

Be honest and if you find you've been missing the boat— turn over a new leaf today!

Relationship Buster!

Criticism is difficult enough, but presented in the presence of others, it can cause lasting damage to a marriage relationship.

If you must correct your spouse, do it only in the safety of your shared aloneness.

Word of Wisdom: Don't be surprised to find that the need to criticize often disappears while you're waiting for an appropriate time to address it.

Words of Wisdom

*Walking Wisely in
Any Relationship*

- Wrap and rewrap your relationships in many layers of forgiveness.

- When you talk about yourself, be willing to open up but not too wide!

_____

• People are like tea bags,
you never know how strong they are
until you see them in hot water.

• Perseverance and determination are critical
to relationships. Without the ability to
"hang in there," the slightest winds
can blow a relationship off course.

_____

• You can give without loving,
but you can't love without giving.

• Love seeks to *make* happy
as well as *be* happy!

————

• Never underestimate the impact of
one kind word!

• Being brutal and being honest
are not the same thing.

————